Twist & Twirl Soft Colored Wire to Make Jewelry & Fun Critters

Tools

Old Scissors, Wire Cutters or Fingernail Clippers

Other Stuff

Dowels

Needle Tool

Skewer

Pencil

Craft Sticks

Sharpie Marker

Knife

Findings

Seed Beads

Wiggle Eyes

Pin Backs

Ear Wires

Toothpicks

Easy Does It Beads...

by E. Wayne Fox

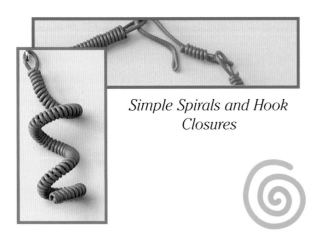

Simple Spirals and Hook Closures

Simple, colorful wire jewelry is so easy! Just fold wire to make a core and then wrap the end of the wire around the core to make a coiled link. Forming loops at the end makes it easy to attach the links to create simple earrings, necklaces and bracelets; just use your imagination. Use our color combinations or create your own to match a wardrobe or your school colors!

Spiral

Step 1. Fold wire to make 3 strands and slip through loop.

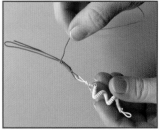

Step 2. Tightly coil end of wire around folded wire

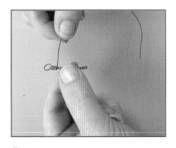

Step 3. Wrap coiled wire around a dowel to make spiral.

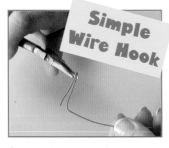

Simple Wire Hook

Step 1. Bend 1½" of wire over with needle-nose pliers.

Step 2. From a small loop with pliers.

Step 3. Wrap wire around bottom of loop several times.

Step 4. Bend loop into a smooth hook.

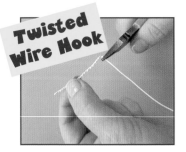

Twisted Wire Hook

Step 1. For hook, double 2" of wire and twist tightly.

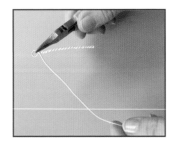

Step 2. Form a small loop at end of twists.

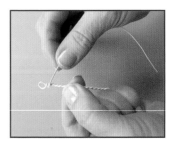

Step 3. Wrap wire around bottom of loop several times

Step 4. Bend wire into a hook with pliers.

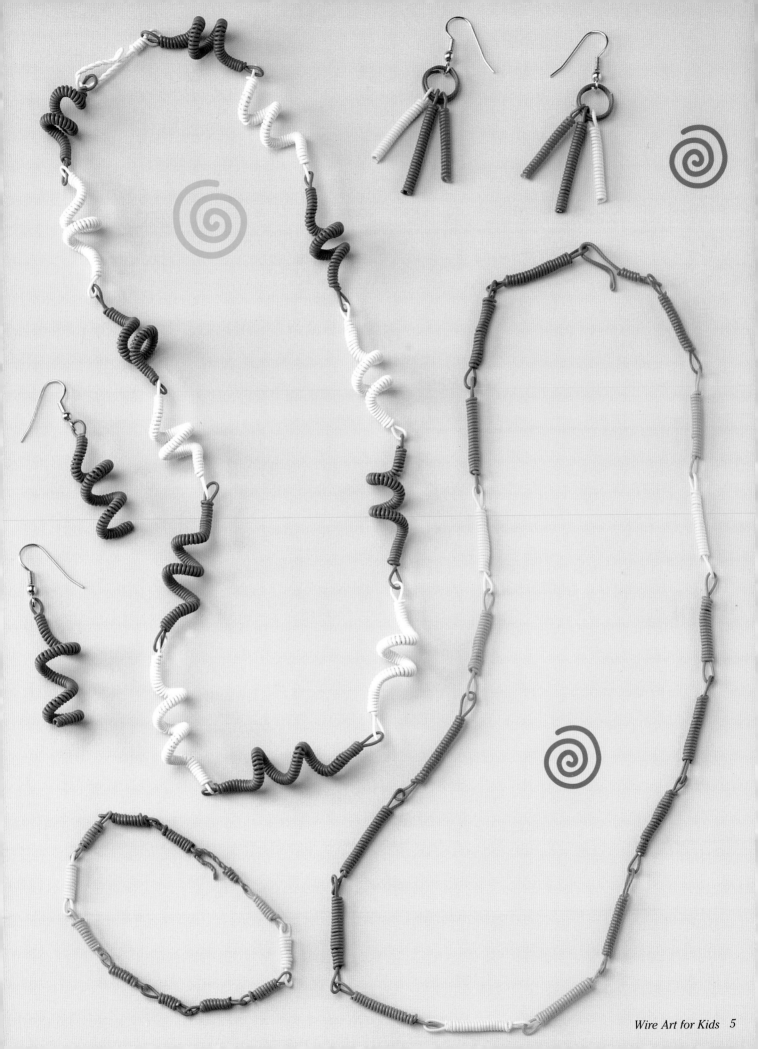

Easy Beads...

by Chris Gluck

Twisted Spirals

Twisted Spirals

Twisted spirals look intricate, but they're simple to make. Just twist wire around a craft stick, slip the wire off the stick and the twists form automatically. Beads are used to add colorful accents and they can cover the twists where the wire ends are joined. With these easy techniques, you can quickly make jewelry for everyone on your gift list!

Step 1. Hold wire in one hand. Leaving a 1" tail, use thumb of other hand to hold wire against craft stick. Wrap wire around stick placing each wrap against the one before until desired length is complete.

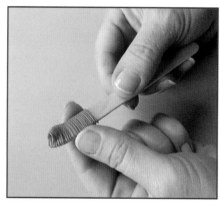

Step 2. Don't wrap wire too tight. If coils are spread out, stop and push wire coils together. When removed from the stick, tension on the wire creates spiral coils.

Step 3. Many other items such as dowels, pencils, meat skewers and crochet hooks, can be used to make coils of different sizes.

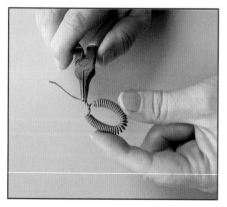

Step 4. Make coil of wire and bend into shape. Twist ends together with pliers.

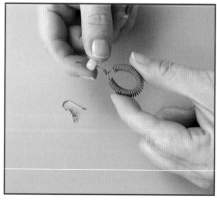

Step 5. Slip beads over wires to cover joints or add as accents.

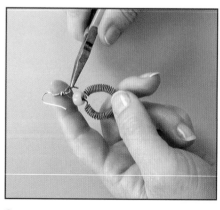

Step 6. Add earring wires or bracelet closures to coiled wire.

Earrings
By Delores Frantz

Easy Beads...

by Chris Gluck

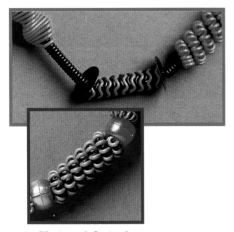

Twisted Spirals

Wire spirals and twists in these great projects. Friends will think you spent a fortune buying your jewelry. And when you say you made it yourself, they'll be amazed!

Coiled Core Wire

Step 1. Make a tight coil of black wire. Wrap coiled wire around dowel to form a spiral.

Step 2. Remove coils from dowel. Slip black coil into center of colored coil.

Crimped Wire

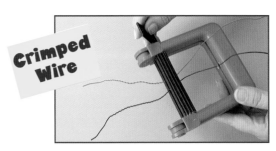

Step 1. For crimped wire, insert wire in a paper crimping tool and turn handle.

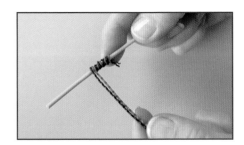

Step 2. Coil crimped wires around a dowel and make a crimped coil.

Wire Core Bead

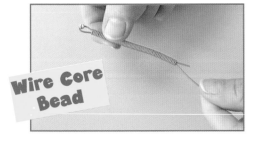

Step 1. Center bead on one color of wire and fold in half. Wrap second color of wire around strands to make coil.

Step 2. Wrap coil around dowel to make a spiral.

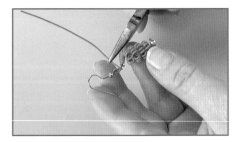

Step 3. Using ends of core wire, attach earring wire.

Twisty Beads

Step 1. Make a twisted spiral following steps 1 and 2 on page 6.

Step 2. Pull to lengthen spiral and form wire into a loose ball.

Step 3. Slip twisty beads onto a wire along with beads and finish with a loop and hook.

Twisty Beads...
by Chris Gluck

and Coils

Add a new twist to your jewelry collection. Twisty beads for barrettes and jewelry are fast and easy!

Twisty Everything

Barrette

Step 1. String beads on wire and wrap around barrette placing beads as shown.

Step 2. Crimp wire and wrap wire between beads in one direction.

Step 3. Wrap in opposite direction and secure end.

Coils & Beads

Step 1. Coil wire around a dowel alternating short coils and loops with beads.

Step 2. Remove wire from dowel and stretch each coiled wire out slightly.

Step 3. Make two sets of coils and beads, twist together.

Step 4. Make a loop in one and a hook on the other end.

More Decor...

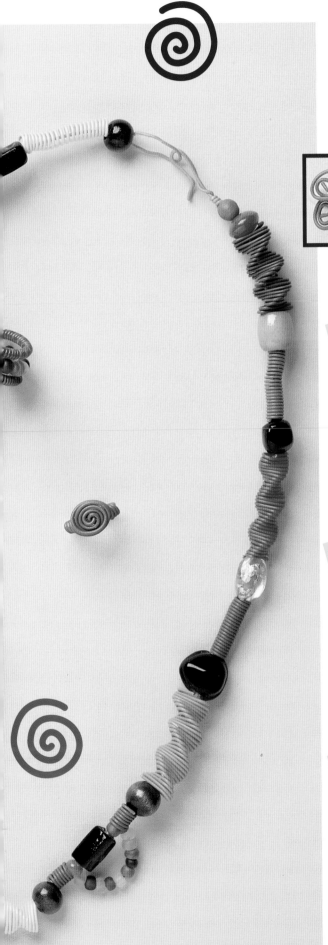

Coils & Spirals

by Chris Gluck

Need a pair of special shades or a just-right piece of jewelry? Try these Wire Art wonders.

Sunglasses

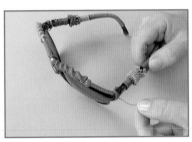

Step 1. String a set of coils and beads long enough to go across top of glasses on wire. Wrap a short piece of wire around center as shown.

Step 2. Twist ends of wire around ear pieces. Make assorted wire coils around straight part of ear pieces and smooth coils around curves.

Necklace

Step 1. Make a coil on a dowel, ad beads to make a loop like you see in the necklace.

Step 2. Coil the other end, trim excess wire. String on a necklace with more beads to fill the center.

Spiral Ring

Step 1. Cut 6" pieces of 3 colors of wire for core. Make a coil around core long enough to fit around finger.

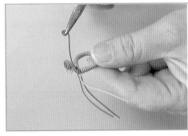

Step 2. Twist core wires together. Trim ends of wires to different lengths and shape into flat spirals.

Wire Creatures...

by Delores Frantz

These happy little guys will light up anyone's smile. Sit them around your favorite room; they look great sitting on top of your computer screen too. Why not make the whole creature collection?

Bunny

Step 1. Make tight coil with 48" of wire and wrap around a ¼" dowel . Bend wire ends into center of coil.

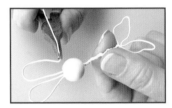

Step 2. Fold 15" of wire in half, shape ears. Twist for 1½" and thread on bead. Shape feet and wrap end around twists.

Step 3. Make coil on 3½" of wire for arms twist center around neck add bead hands. Pull feet out into position.

Bee

Step 1. Make tight yellow and black coils. Cut to the proper lengths with wire cutter.

Step 2. Center first coil on black wire, pass ends of wire through second coil in opposite directions.

Step 3. Add rest of body coils passing ends of wire through in opposite directions.

Step 4. Thread on head bead. Trim off excess wire and shape antennae.

Step 5. Make a tight coil of wire and form into figure eight for wings.

Step 6. Glue wing to back of bee with hot glue.

Dragonfly

Step 1. Fold wire and make a coil around strands. Thread on head bead.

Step 2. Trim ends of wire and shape antennae with needle nose pliers.

Step 3. Make 2 tight coils of wire and form into figure eights for wings.

Step 4. Cross wings at center and glue to back of fly.

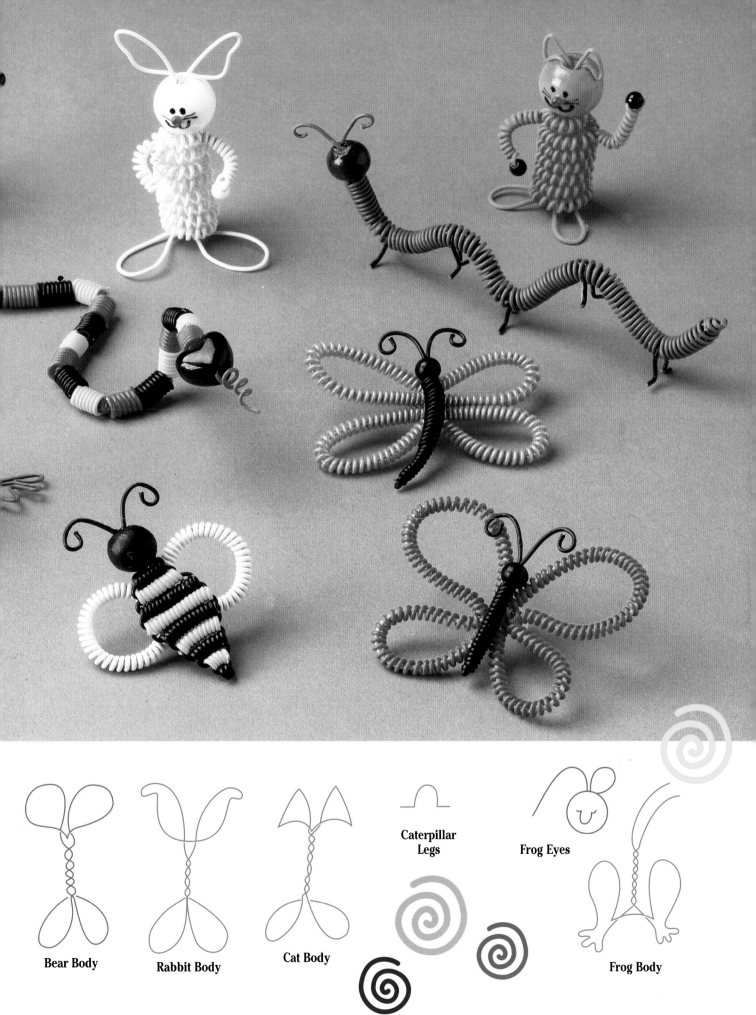

Bear Body

Rabbit Body

Cat Body

Caterpillar Legs

Frog Eyes

Frog Body

Step 1. Form wire into shape. Fold wire at bottom of legs. Add extra pieces for tail.

Step 2. Wrap Black wire around back legs and base of the tail.

Step 3. Wrap Black wire around body, front legs, neck and head.

Step 4. Wrap Silver wire around horse. Shape the tail and mane.

Wire Horses & People

Form & Shape

by Chris Gluck

Create whimsical people and their fantasy mounts. They're as much fun to make as they are to receive. Start making some today!

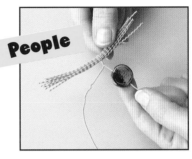

Step 1. Cut lengths of crimped wire. Twist a piece of wire around center and thread on a flat bead for face. Twist.

Step 2. Thread on disk bead for neck. Separate wires. Twist wire.

Step 3. Make a coil on a dowel and slide onto wire for arms. Thread on hand bead and pass wire back through arm.

Step 4. Make twisted spiral coil for body. Separate wires for legs.

Step 5. Make a twisted spiral coil for each leg. Thread on spiral coil and a foot bead, wrap wire up around the 'ankle' and cut off excess.

People

Making The Horse
1. Start with one wire 2' long.
2. & 3. Form ears; make two small loops.
4. & 5. Form front legs and wrap each end once in the center. Twist the wire to form the back.
6. & 7. Form back legs and twist at center.
8. The remaining wire forms the tail.

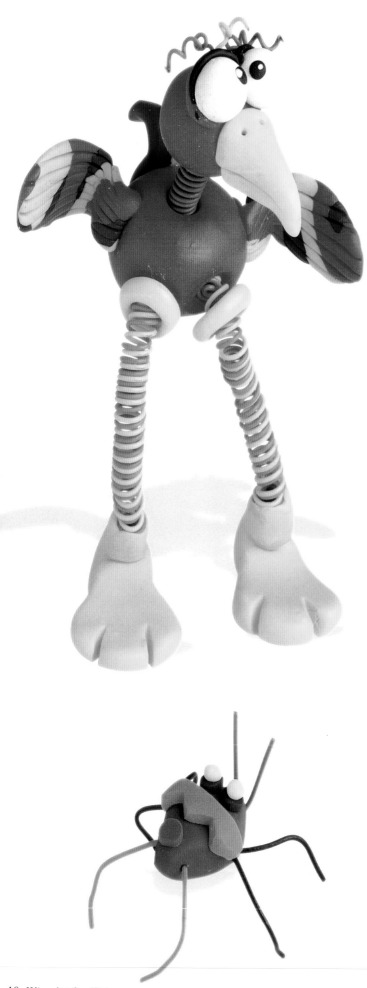

What You'll Need:

Wire

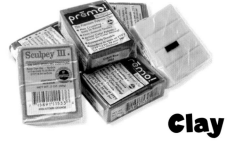

Clay

Tools

Needle Tool

Dowels

Skewer

Pencil

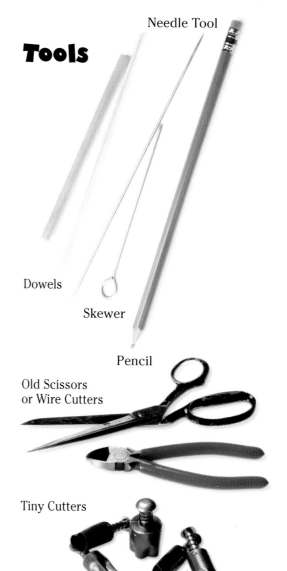

Old Scissors
or Wire Cutters

Tiny Cutters

Wire & Clay...

Bitsy Bugs...

by Mary Harrison

Easy as 1 . 2 . 3 !

Always do a test first to see how long your wire can be baked in the clay before melting. Some wire cannot be baked higher than 265°F for more than 10 minutes.

Step 1. Shape and attach body parts. Begin with balls of clay and flatten slightly as you shape. Press shapes together.

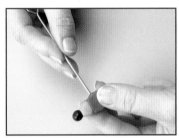

Step 2. Place in freezer for 10 minutes. Remove one at a time and make holes for legs and antennae with needle tool.

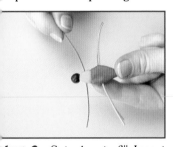

Step 3. Cut wires to 6". Insert wires through bodies for legs and antennae. Note: Do not cut wires too short, the plastic coating shrinks during baking.

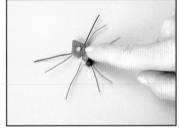

Step 4. Decorate body with dots and zig zags. See the techniques below. Place dots and zig zags on body and press gently to attach.

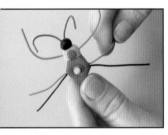

Step 5. Separate legs before baking to keep them from sticking together. Bake bugs at 265°F for 12 minutes. Trim and shape legs and antennae

Dots 1. Roll a thin snake of clay. Place in the freezer for 5 minutes to harden. Remove from freezer and slice into small dots.

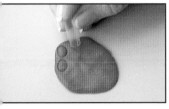

Dots 2. Roll out a sheet of clay and cut out dots shapes with a drinking straw or other tool.

Zig Zags. Roll out a sheet of clay and cut out strips with decorative scissors.

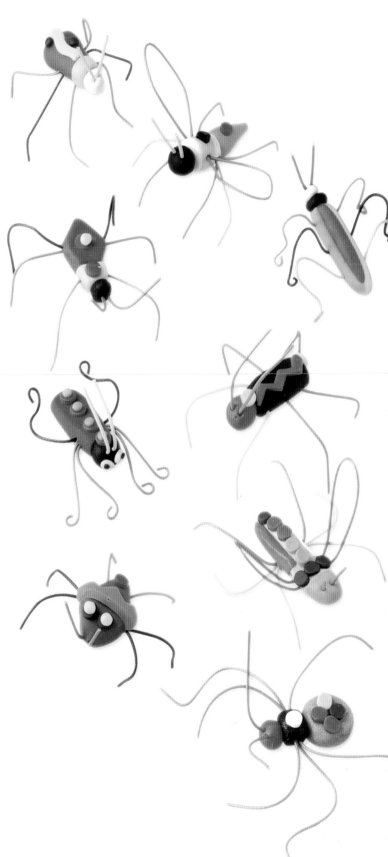

Easy Beads & Wire...

Wire & Beads

By Lisa Pavelka

Beads & Twists

Intricate beads are simple and quick to make with easy to handle polymer clay.

Smiley Faces

Step 1. Roll a ball of yellow clay, flatten into a disk. Shape face parts from black clay, place on disk and press into place.

Twisted Beads

Step 1. Roll out thin logs of 2 different colors of clay. Lightly twist logs together.

Step 2. Roll twisted log to lengthen and blend colors.

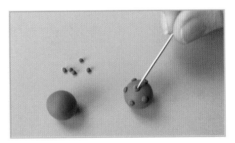

Step 3. Fold log in half and twist into a teardrop shape.

Ball Beads

Step 1. Roll a clay log and cut off small pieces with a plastic knife. Roll into balls.

Step 2. For dotted balls, roll tiny balls of clay, place on larger ball with a needle tool and lightly press in place.

Clay Wrap Beads

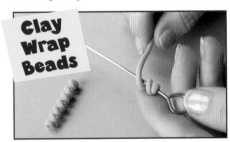

Step 1. Roll out thin log of clay and coil into a spiral around a skewer or dowel.

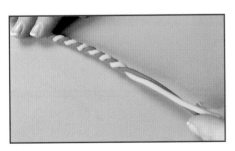

Step 2. For 2 color beads, roll thin logs of 2 different colors and twist together.

Step 3. Roll twisted log to lengthen and blend colors.

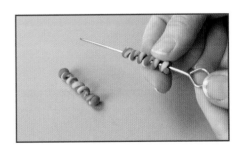

Step 4. Coil log into a spiral around a skewer or dowel. Bake on skewer.

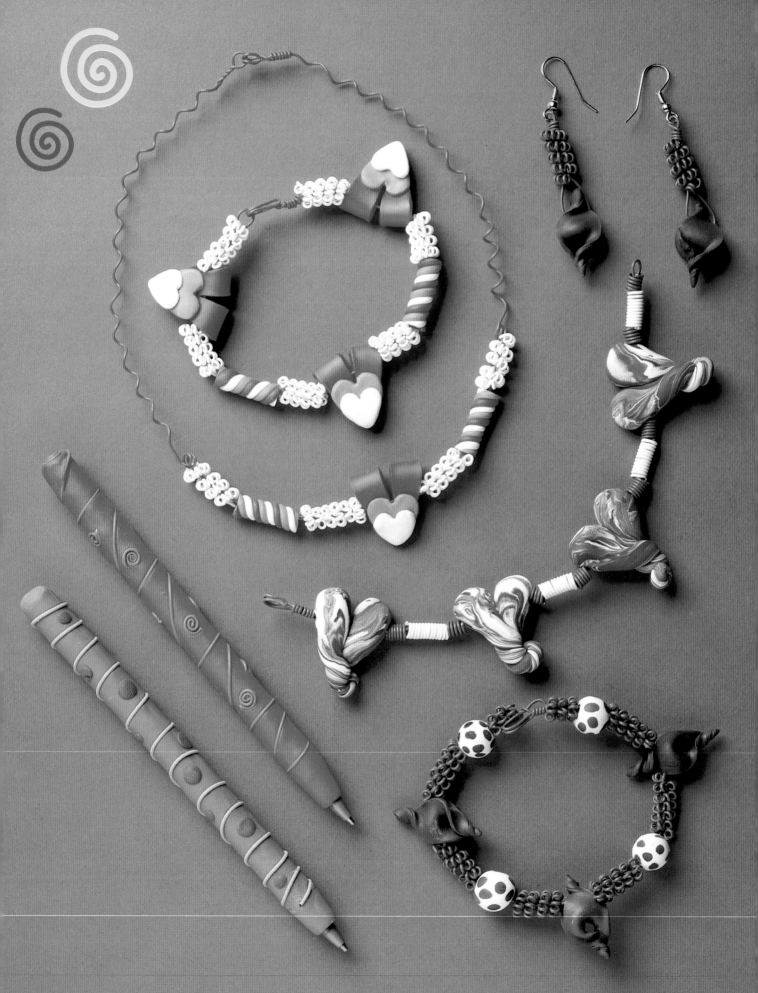

More Beads & Wire...

Wire Wrap & Twirl

by Lisa Pavelka

Make beads from wire and from clay then combine them into jewelry pieces you'll be proud to wear or give!

Beads & Twists

Wire Coil Pens *by E. Wayne Fox*
Remove ink cartridge from pen. Roll a sheet of clay and wrap the pen. Wrap with wire. Add clay dots or spirals. Bake.

Candy Cane Beads

Step 1. Roll thin logs of 3 different colors of clay. Place side by side.

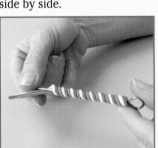

Step 2. Coil logs around a skewer or dowel keeping colors separate and parallel.

Step 3. Cut coil to length with a craft knife.

Flower Beads

Step 1. For a round bead, roll a ball of clay, add tiny balls of a second color and roll lightly.

Step 2. For a tube bead, roll a log of clay, place on skewer and cut to length. Roll tiny balls on other colors, stack of bead and roll lightly. Bake on Skewer.

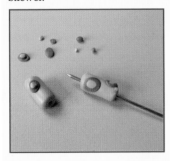

Step 3. For flowers, use a tiny cutter and pick up with a pin. Place on ball and roll lightly.

Twisted Teardrop Beads

Step 1. Roll thin sheets of clay and cut out squares with a small cutter.

Step 2. Fold squares into triangles. Curve the top, pinch together and twist.

Step 3. Blend 3 colors of clay together and shape into 2 long teardrops. Twist together.

Folded Heart Beads

Step 1. Cut hearts from 2 colors of clay using small and tiny cutters.

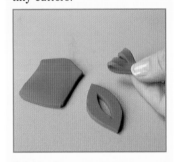

Step 2. Roll a thin sheet of clay and cut out a piece shaped like lips. Fold in half.

Step 3. Stack small and tiny heart shapes and press in place as shown.

Pencil Toppers
By Lisa Pavelka

Garden Critters...
Roll & Cut

By E. Wayne Fox

This is truly a snake of a different hue! He's really a necklace designed just for you. Or, if you'd rather, make one of his companions to brighten your day.

Octopus

Step 1. Shape balls and face parts from clay. Make coils of wire for legs. Assemble referring to photo and bake.

Bee

Step 1. Roll a sheet of white clay and cut out wings with a small teardrop cutter.

Step 2. Make a log of yellow clay and coil around pencil to make hive. Make a small coil of yellow wire.

Step 3. Roll balls of clay for body and antennae and make coils of black wire. Assemble referring to photo, bake.

Snake

Step 1. Shape head from Green clay, add tiny Purple balls for eyes, cut mouth and make holes for eyes. Shape Red wire tongue, insert in mouth. Make coils of Green wire around a pencil.

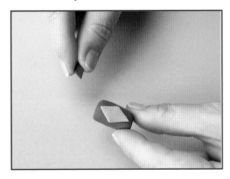

Step 2. Make 5 tube beads. Roll thin sheets of Yellow and Purple clay, cut out diamonds and press in place on beads. Top with Green dot.

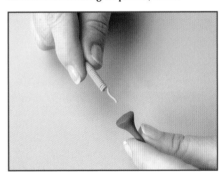

Step 3. For tail, make a Green clay teardrop and a thin coil of Yellow wire. Insert end of coil in bead. Assemble necklace referring to photo, bake.

Lady Bug

Step 1. Roll a Red ball for body and Black clay for face, flatten slightly. Roll thin log for stripe.

Step 2. Make tiny Black wire coils and clay balls for antennae. Roll tiny White balls for eyes.

Step 3. Roll tiny Black balls for spots, place on body and flatten. Assemble referring to photo. Press on pencil, remove and bake.

Step 4. Roll out Pink and Yellow clay, cut out flowers. Add center dots.

Step 5. Insert stems into flowers and and bake. Twist stems together.

Step 6. Roll clay and cut out heart with a tiny cutter.

Flowers & Vines...

Wire & Clay Combinations

By syndee holt

Hearts and flowers, vine and leaves...these bright creations can be used in a variety of ways...trim a frame, top a pencil or make a necklace. Make one for yourself or make them all for gifts!

Step 1. Roll out a thin sheet of Green clay.

Step 2. Cut out leaves. Add vein marks with needle tool.

Step 3. Cut out flowers with a tiny cutter and cut stems from wire.

Step 7. Insert wire stems into hearts and bake.

Step 8. Twist stems together. Assemble vine or necklace.

Step 9. Insert wires in stars then in ball of clay for pencil topper, bake.

Sunny Day...

By Lisa Pavelka

Sun

Step 1. Roll out sheets of Yellow and Orange and cut out circles.

Birdhouse

Step 1. Roll white clay and cut out house. Mark lines with plastic knife.

Love Birds

Step 1. Roll balls of Yellow and Orange. Flatten Orange balls and shape feet. Make coils of wire for legs.

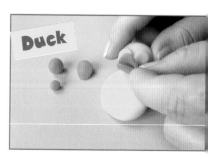

Duck

Step 1. Roll balls of orange and Yellow, flatten and arrange as shown.

Every day is a sunny day when these projects brighten your way. Birds feel right at home as they roam freely under the sun.

Step 2. Stack circles and cut out notches. Coil wire for stem.

Step 3. Twist each ray twice. Insert and stretch out stem.

Step 4. Draw face with a fine tip permanent marker.

Step 2. Roll Red teardrops, flatten for shingles. Make Black hole and press in place. Cut toothpick for perch.

Step 3. Roll Blue teardrops and balls for bird. Make Yellow beak. Assemble referring to photo and bake.

Birdhouse Pattern

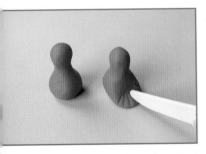

Step 2. Make a pear shape from Red or Blue clay. Flatten bottom and mark tail feathers with plastic knife.

Step 3. Roll balls, shape teardrop, flatten and mark feathers. Wrap wings around body. Make Yellow beak.

Step 4. Roll yellow balls, flatten and cut toes. Make coils of wire for legs and insert in feet. Assemble bird, bake.

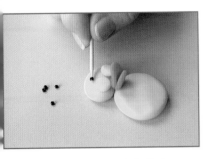

Step 2. Roll tiny Black balls for eyes and place with toothpick.

Step 3. Roll ball, shape teardrop, flatten and mark feathers with paper clip.

It's Raining Cats & Dogs... *By Lisa Pavelka*

Roll, Flatten, Shape, Assemble & Bake

Gather your clay, wire and a few around-the-house tools to make these delightful works of art for kids ages 9 - 95!

Rainbow

Step 1. Roll 3 White balls of clay. Stack and flatten bottom slightly.

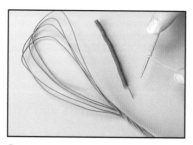

Step 2. Make 6 rainbow color coils of wire around a skewer.

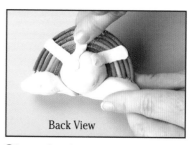

Back View

Step 3. Assemble rainbow and clouds as shown and bake.

Dog

Step 1. Roll White ball and flatten for body . Draw spots with permanent marker. Make parts for collar.

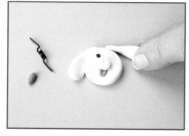

Step 2. Make White teardrops for ears, Black balls for eyes, Pink oval for mouth and wire coil for neck.

Step 3. Roll White balls for feet and flatten. Make wire coils for legs and insert in feet and body.

Step 4. Roll White ball and shape teardrop. Make wire coil for tail. Assemble, draw dots and bake.

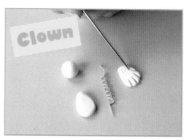

Clown

Step 1. Roll White balls, flatten and mark fingers with needle tool. Make coils of wire for arms.

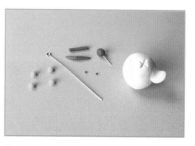

Step 2. Roll balls for head parts. and arrange referring to photo. Insert Red map pin for nose.

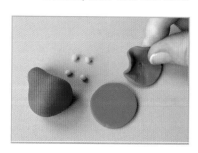

Step 3. Make a Red pear shape for body, Yellow balls for spots and Green circle for collar. Ruffle collar.

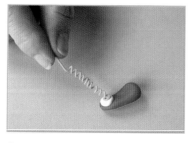

Step 4. Make Red teardrops and White balls for shoes and socks. Coil Yellow wire for clown legs. Assemble and bake.

Cat

Step 1. Roll a thin strip of White clay and cut out triangles with a craft knife.

Rainbow
By E. Wayne Fox

Step 2. Roll a ball of White, flatten and cut out fish. Make a coil of White wire.

Step 3. Make face. Crimp White wire and make whiskers. Insert trimmed ball head pins for eyes.

Step 4. Insert whiskers. Assemble cat and fish referring to photo. and bake to finish.

Fish Pattern

Looney Birds...

By Kris Richards

Cock-eyed looney birds to tickle your funny bone and delight even the oldest child you know.

Step 2. Insert legs and Blue coil for neck in body ball.

Step 3. Shape feet and cut toes. Make holes with toothpick.

Step 4. Insert legs into feet.

Step 5. Insert neck coil into head ball. Press both into body.

Step 7. Shape a Yellow cone for beak and make holes.

Step 8. Make eyes, add Black pupils and tiny highlights.

Step 9. Roll 3 colors into ball. Make tail and wings.

Step 10. Insert wire coils into top of head for feathers.

Step 2. Flatten and shape feet. Mark toes with needle tool or toothpick.

Step 3. Press ball for body on top of feet.

Step 4. Insert wire coil for neck into body.

Step 5. Press ball for head on top of neck coil.

Step 7. Make eyes, add Black pupils and tiny highlights.

Step 8. Roll thin logs of 3 colors and press together.

Step 9. Roll to form log and blend colors.

Step 10. Fold clay in half and twist together. Bake.

Step 12. Shape pieces into teardrops and draw lines.

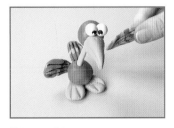

Step 13. Press tail and wings into place on body.

Step 14. Insert wire coils for feathers into top of head. Bake.

Crazy Critters...

By Kris Richards

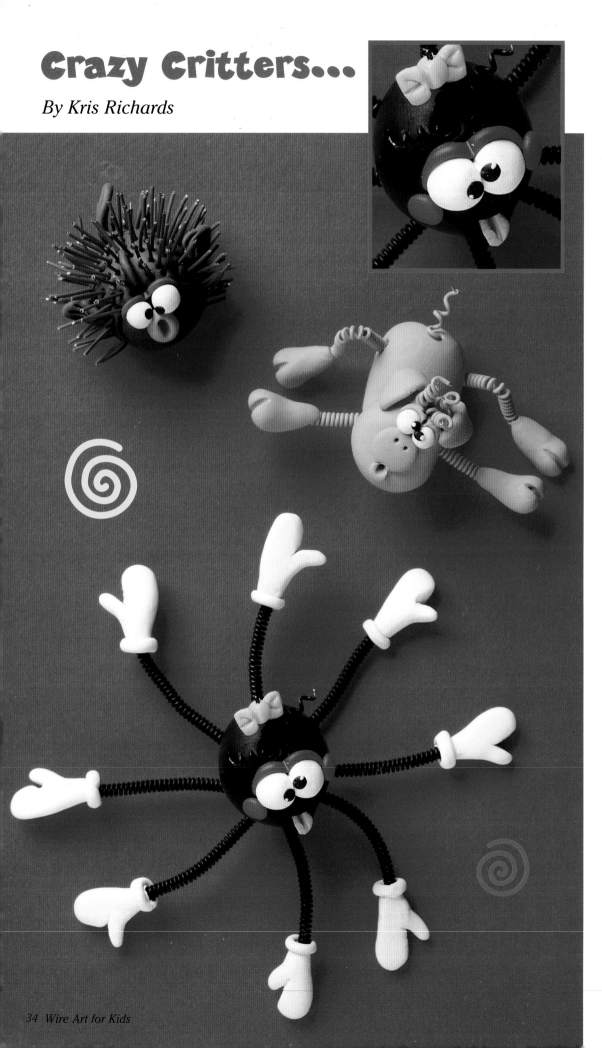